Folds of skin on a bat's face help the bat make squeaking sounds.

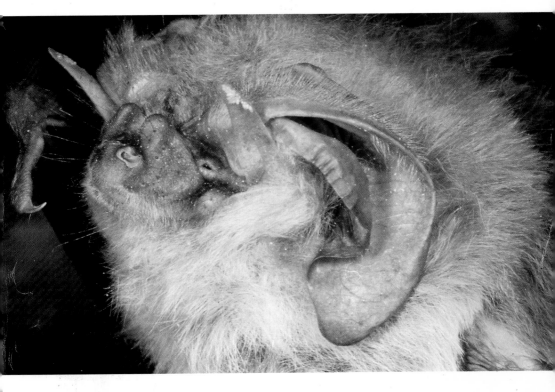

Try using different faces to help you make different sounds.

3

Are these birds?

No, they are *mammals* called bats.
Bats are the only mammals that fly.

Like all mammals, bats have hair.

Like all mammals, baby bats can drink milk from their mothers.

Why are all these bats
upside down?

Bats hang upside down to rest.

Bats rest on a *roost*.

A roost can be a tree, a cave, or an attic.

A bat's strong toes have
sharp claws.

These strong toes can hold on
to a roost all day long!

The squeaking sounds bounce
off an insect.

se sounds come back
e bat as *echoes*.

Bats rest during the day.

They are *nocturnal*. Nocturnal
animals are awake at night.

These bats leave their roosts
every night to hunt for insects.

To find insects, bats use
echolocation.

First a bat makes high
squeaking sounds.

The
to th

The echoes tell the bat
where the insect is.

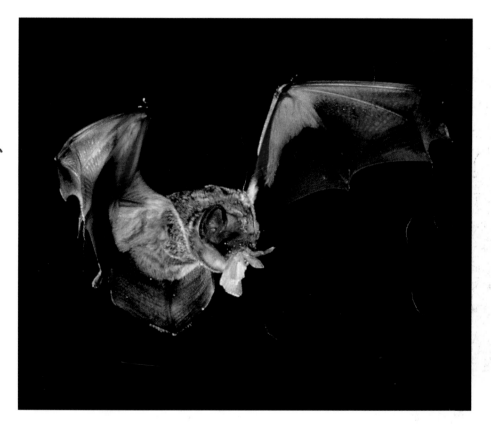

How would you make an echo?

Some bats squeak through their noses!

Just like you, bats need
to drink water.

Some bats also drink *nectar*
from flowers. Nectar is sweet.

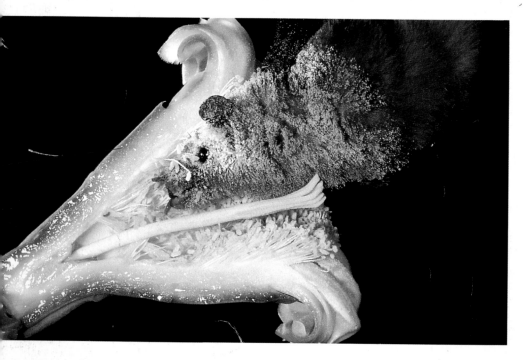

Bats carry yellow *pollen*
from flower to flower.
Pollen helps flowers make seeds.

Watch out!

Some snakes eat bats.

Look closely at the wings of this bat.

Each wing is made of an arm
and a hand.

Thin skin joins the arm
and four fingers.

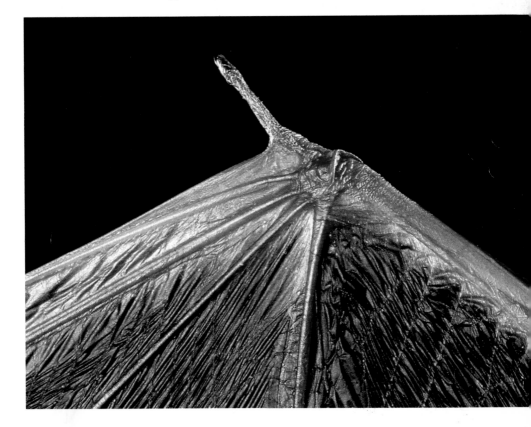

The thumb sticks out alone.

Baby bats are called *pups.*

Some pups live in safe places called *nurseries.*

This mother is searching for her pup.

How will she ever find it?

A mother bat knows the sound
and smell of her own pup.

Look! She has found it.

Some pups ride on their mothers' backs.

Who gives you piggyback rides?

Squeaking bats eat insects.

Bats also help flowers grow.

Bats do jobs that help our whole world.

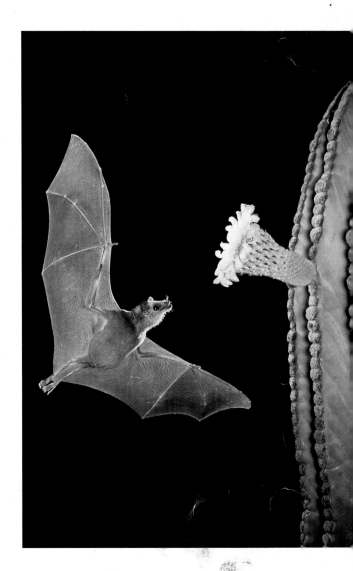

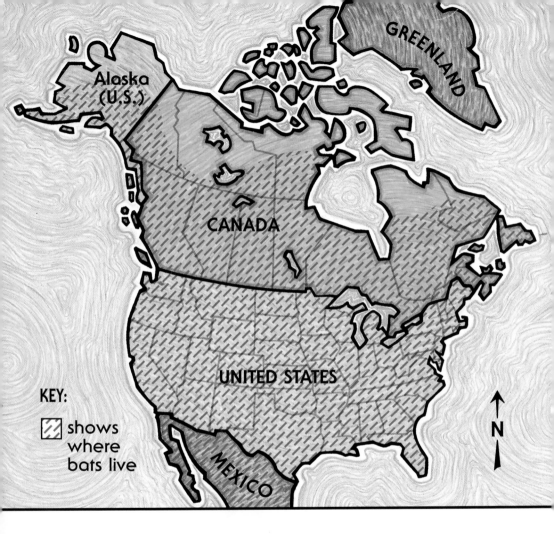

Find your state or province on this map.
Do bats live near you?

Parts of a Bat's Body

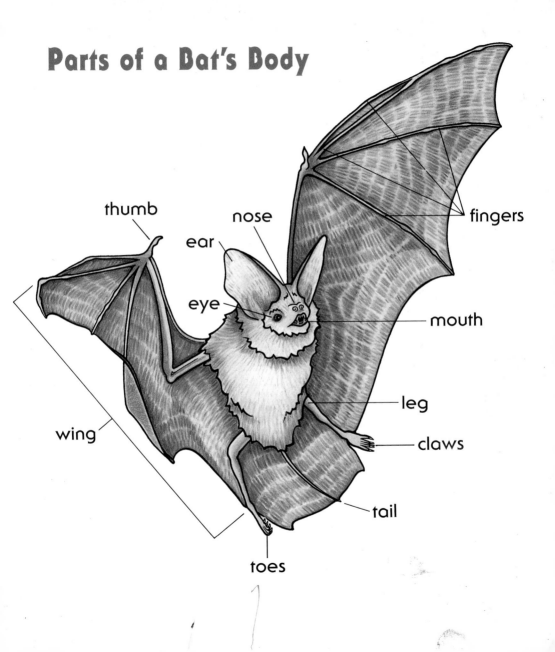

thumb

nose

ear

fingers

eye

mouth

leg

claws

wing

tail

toes

Glossary

echoes: repeated sounds that have bounced off an object

echolocation: finding an object by using echoes

mammals: animals that have hair and drink mother's milk when young. (Some mammals are humans, bears, wolves, bats, and whales.)

nectar: a sweet liquid made in flowers

nocturnal: active at night

nurseries: safe places where some baby animals grow up

pollen: yellow powder that helps flowers make seeds

pups: baby bats

roost: a place where bats rest

Hunt and Find

The publisher wishes to extend special thanks to our **series consultant,** Sharyn Fenwick. An elementary science-math specialist, Mrs. Fenwick was the recipient of the National Science Teachers Association 1991 Distinguished Teaching Award. In 1992, representing the state of Minnesota at the elementary level, she received the Presidential Award for Excellence in Math and Science Teaching.

About the Author

Robin Buckley

Ruth Berman was born in New York and grew up in Minnesota. As a child, she spent her time going to school and saving lost and hurt animals. Later, Ruth volunteered at three zoos and got her degree in English. She enjoys writing science books for children. She has written six books in Lerner's Pull Ahead series. Her other books include *Ants, Peacocks,* and *My Pet Dog* (Lerner Publications) and *Sharks* and *American Bison* (Carolrhoda Books). Ruth lives in California with her dog, Hannah, and her two cats, Nikki and Toby.

Photo Acknowledgments

The photographs in this book are reproduced through the courtesy of: © Merlin D. Tuttle, Bat Conservation International, front and back covers, pages 4–6, 8–9, 11, 13–21, 23–27, 31; © Robert and Linda Mitchell, pages 3, 7, 10, 12, 22.